The Mindset of Retirement Success

"In *The Mindset of Retirement Success*, Friedman delivers a cogent, implementable framework of habits and best practices for securing one's financial future. I highly recommend this book."

—**Glenn Sabin,** Author of *n of 1: One Man's Harvard-Documented Remission of Incurable Cancer Using Only Natural Methods,* Founder, FON Consulting

"Rodger Friedman provides the tools we need to plan a retirement we can enjoy without the worries of financial restraint. I wish I had this book much earlier in my career, but I will be SURE to share it with my children! Starting early, with a sound financial plan, instead of just hoping it works out, makes a lot more sense!"

—**Dr. Judy Morgan** DVM, CVA, CVCP, CVFT
Nationally renowned author and veterinarian
Author of *From Needles to Natural* and *Canine Kitchen Capers*

"Thanks to Rodger Friedman's book *The Mindset of Retirement Success*, you can stop worrying about retirement and start preparing. Rodger shows you how to stop feeling overwhelmed and begin to make major progress in this important area for you and your family."

—**Steve Harrison,** VP Bradley Communications
Co-founder BestsellerBlueprint.com

"This practical book gives you a step by step process to help achieve financial independence and organize your life so you can enjoy your dream retirement."

—**Brian Tracy,** Best Selling Author, Professional Speaker, Entrepreneur and Success Expert, President and CEO Brian Tracy International

"In this best practices manual, Friedman lays out concrete steps you can follow to increase your chances for retirement prosperity. In plain English, he tells you what you need to do. If after reading this book, you are not motivated to fully prepare for your retirement, there must be something wrong with you."

—**Dr. Arturo Betancourt** M.D., F.A.C.S. is a Comprehensive Ophthalmologist, Cataract & LASIK eye surgeon at Baltimore Washington Eye Center. Dr. Betancourt is the President and Medical Director of Baltimore Washington Eye Center

"Rodger Friedman hits a home run with *The Mindset of Retirement Success.* He explains step by step the ideal path to follow if you want to intelligently prepare for a financially secure retirement. Rodger not only explains the steps, but also, the "why" and reasoning behind each step. This helps keep us on track for financial security."

—**Dr. George Flinn Jr. was a 2016** Republican **candidate** to the U.S. House **to represent** the 8th Congressional District of Tennessee. Dr. Flinn is a practicing radiologist and the owner of Flinn Broadcasting, which has over 40 radio and television stations throughout the country. George Flinn is the founder and president of The Flinn Clinic in Memphis Tennessee.

"The Mindset of Retirement Success addresses an issue that so many of us put on the back burner, never to address until it's too late. Rodger does a fabulous job pointing out that we, ultimately, are the ones who have to push ourselves to plan for our future or we only have ourselves to blame. 54321...call your financial advisor today!"

—**Mel Robbins,** International Best Selling Author of *The 5 Second Rule,* contributing editor to *SUCCESS* magazine, CNN commentator

"Rodger Friedman's book is replete with practical ideas to help a person prepare for retirement. Suggestions such as his should be part of a personal finance course that all high school students in the USA should be required to take."

—**Dr. Alan Goodwin,** Principal, Walt Whitman High School, Bethesda MD

"During my thirty-five-year career of advising business owners, the most difficult task I have had has been persuading them that they needed to be preparing right now for financial independence. How I wish this book had been available to them decades ago! It is brief, friendly, and easy to understand. Read it now and apply its lessons. Your future self will be so grateful!"

—**Roberta A. Grimes**, Esq. Author, Business Attorney and Consultant

"There are thousands of books offering investment advice to people planning their retirement. This book is different in that it focuses on the mindset required to succeed. This is the perfect book to help you get started on the right path."

—**Jamie Stone,** Certified Public Accountant (CPA) Partner, JD, LLM, Heymann, Suissa & Stone, PC

"This book is a great book. Rodger has an ability to make a retirement book interesting and readable. Reading this book can change your entire perspective on retirement planning."
—**Michael A. Reeder**, CPA

"Rodger's clear, concise and simplistic description to prepare for retirement creates a breakthrough for the reader. Investing and preparing for the future is an idea that many feel is impossible, complicated or a missed opportunity. Rodger outlines an ideal path for a mindset of preparation towards a successful retirement. "

—**Dr. Nancy Fox,** Author, Speaker, Life Strategist, Founder Red Tale Fox Enterprises

The Mindset of
RETIREMENT
SUCCESS

The Mindset of
RETIREMENT
SUCCESS

7 Winning Strategies to Change Your Life

RODGER ALAN FRIEDMAN

ISBN: 978-0-9996414-0-8

This book is dedicated to my wife, Reena Friedman, who encourages me to continue spreading the word that a financially secure retirement is possible for many if they would only make it a focus. Reena is the light of my life and has put up with me for 26 years. Thank you for being my partner through this wonderful adventure we call marriage. I love you.

Table of Contents

Foreword

By John Henry Lambert

When Rodger asked me if I would write the forward for his third book, I thought, "What an honor! What a challenge! Where do I start?" As a musician, what can I say about someone I've known for 50 years who has attained success far beyond all the folks we grew up with? What do I know about money and finance? I spent decades learning music—that I know. Money? Not so much.

How many sleepovers did we have in 1968? It's hard to say. Our parents couldn't keep us apart. There we were, Johnnie and Rodger, two 12-year-old troublemakers. We were students at P.S.40 on the lower east side of New York City, trying to survive through Mrs. Baker's 6th grade home room class, along with a cast of other characters that we called our teachers. I smile looking at our 6th grade class picture—dressed in sport jackets our moms bought us at Barney Boys Town. Rodger and I both wore cranberry jackets and looked like bookends. We were city kids, growing up like weeds somewhere between Greenwich Village and the Empire State Building.

This was our tromping ground. Not bad. We were in a place where we could either sink or swim, and I thank God every day that little Johnnie and Rodger had parents who helped us swim—parents who cared for and loved us. Even before 7th grade, we both experienced the reality of life: death visited our families. The passing of Rodger's mom and the passing of my younger brother Jimmie hit us hard. But we had each other to lean on, and life continued. We gathered strength from each other. Our carefree existence in the seemingly safe surroundings of our hood came to a grinding halt. Like it or not, we had just grown up...fast! After school we went to work for our dads, me in Gramercy Park and Rodger at his dad's Time Square laundry.

We nevertheless shared all our experiences, and our friends drew closer to us as time went on. I became entrenched in music, heading uptown to the High School of Music & Art, while Rodger took the downtown bus to Seward Park High School (whose only claim to fame was a former student by the name of Tony Curtis). There was drama, and there were girls...and so on and so on.

Although many years and life's circumstances drew us apart, Rodger always held a special place in my heart, and the same was in reverse. Somehow we had *Forged Bonds of Steel* that stood the test of time (that idea eventually became the title of Rodger's first book).

Fast forward to 2017 (2018 will make 50 years of friendship), Rodger and Johnnie have seen a lot more of life at this point, and a lot more of reality. As a musician, I have no regrets for following my heart; music is my life and my world. I have studied it for decades. Thinking back to dozens of conversations with Rodger, I know that he has studied retirement planning and investing for decades. I believe it is fair to say that the two of us are quite knowledgeable in our respective fields. However, I haven't written a book—or two, or three! But, I have conducted orchestras on the main stage at Lincoln Center and Saint Patrick's Cathedral.

Yet with all my experience in music, I sure wish Rodger had written this book 20 years ago. I would have read it over and over again, letting the concepts sink into my brain and marinate for a while. You best pay attention to the pages that follow and be prepared to take plenty of notes!

This book helps us—yes, you and I—to understand that *resourcefulness* is more important than simply *having resources*. Very few of us will ever hold a winning lottery ticket or receive a substantial inheritance. Rodger explains the importance of getting serious about funding your retirement *today*; that no matter where you are in your career or how old you are, it's never too late to *start*. Having *some* assets earmarked for retirement is light-years better than having none. I only wish we could have had this sort of conversation back in 1968 when we were 13 years old. Had I been saving and investing tiny bits of my income as far back as 50 years ago, I'd be a gazillionaire today (okay, that may be a stretch; but, without a shadow of doubt, I would be in a *far* better place today). Rodger's words on this subject are extremely helpful and easy to understand (even for a prideful musician such as myself).

Pride is an interesting concept. Maybe I was too proud to consider investing, because I thought I was going to be so successful as a musician that I wouldn't need to worry about money later in life. My advice is this: put your pride aside. Don't be so foolish as to believe you couldn't possibly fall short of your lucrative financial dreams, and don't ever assume that money is somehow going to start pouring down from heaven.

In a moment of nostalgia, I'm reminded of a 1936 song by Arthur Johnson and Johnny Burke. One of my favorites, "Pennies from Heaven."

Oh every time it rains
It rains pennies from heaven
Don't you know each cloud contains
Pennies from heaven
You'll find your fortune
Fallin' all over town
Be sure that your umbrella is upside down
Trade them for a package of sunshine and flowers
It you want the things you love
You must have showers
So when you hear it thunder
Don't run under a tree
There'll be pennies from heavenFor you and me...

Perhaps you remember this song sung by Frank Sinatra, Bing Crosby, Dean Martin and Billie Holiday.

And if you invest some of those pennies over the long haul—and follow Rodger's advice in the following pages—you may just realize your retirement dreams.

John Henry Lambert, Jr.
Founder and Music Director
Gramercy Brass Orchestra of New York / A not for profit 501C3 organization serving our communities with quality live music and music education programs for young people since 1982.
www.gramercybrass.org

Preface

Over the next five years, millions of Americans will reach retirement age with little or no retirement savings and no plan for how to generate a lifestyle-sustaining income. I don't want you to be one of them. As I was considering the idea of writing this, my 3rd book, I sat and thought about the thousands of books in the marketplace focusing on investments and retirement. Because there is so much information available in the marketplace, it obviously is not a *lack* of information that causes one to have a poor financial situation. Rather, it is putting the information to use. That has everything to do with one's mindset and willingness to take necessary actions. This book will focus on your willingness and mindset to put in motion the strategies you will need to retire with dignity and adequate financial resources.

My purpose in writing this is to provide you with key ideas, concepts, and strategies that may improve your chances of a financially successful exit from the workforce. I hope to make it exceedingly clear in the pages to come that you cannot dabble your way to retirement. The steps I will share with you may seem simple, but they are not easy. If you want proof, just look around you. The sobering reality is that almost everyone with whom you come in contact either has money problems or is in debt.

Use this book as a resource to help guide you to make better decisions for your future. You will face unforeseen obstacles on the path to a financially secure retirement; my hope is that you do not become your own obstacle. In other words, do not become your own worst enemy due to inappropriate behaviors and actions. I will not lecture you, but I will ask you to think in new ways. Spend time and review the practical pointers embedded throughout these pages and apply them to your financial life.

If you read the popular media, you're aware that there is a "retirement crisis" in America. Simply put, a vast number of people have either been unwilling or unable to save money for their own retirement. Yet, you will find advertisements everywhere enticing you to

Hey honey, maybe we should go in.

purchase one retirement investment or another, enjoy 50 free trades if only you open an account with $25,000, or perhaps no fee and no cost IRA accounts. The *retirement conversation* is alive and well in the media with large numbers of financial institutions positioning themselves to get a share of the hundreds of billions of dollars at stake. The retirement crisis will not be solved by no-fee IRA accounts or 50 free trades. What may help improve the situation is a change of behavior in the retirement-minded investor.

Throughout this book, I will challenge you to become smarter about money. In the final section of this book, I will provide you with additional resources to assist you.

With that in mind, let's talk about creating a financially strong retirement for you. First, let's define terms. What is a financially strong retirement? I think of it as that period of your life where you work only if it satisfies a desire other than a need for money. It is a time where you are able to spend your days fulfilling lifetime ambitions that there never seemed to be enough time for when you were working for a paycheck. Whether it is volunteering, sharing your knowledge as a teacher or coach or starting an entirely new venture just for the sheer challenge of it, or whether it is learning to build handmade furniture or restoring sports cars from your childhood—the point is that you want to be free to pursue whatever excites and interests you.

Introduction

Dan Sullivan taught me that my future is *my property;* it is mine to do with as I choose. It exists in my mind and I can shape and mold it to fit my personal goals and desires. Over the last 15 years, I have created a big future in my thoughts, and now I work daily to turn that into my reality. Now, it's *your turn.* You can create a BIG vision for your retirement that you can make real in *your* mind. Once this vision becomes real on the inside, you can work to make it real on the outside. You want to become a *belief magnet* that attracts people and circumstances into your life to help you construct your big future.

You will want to create a shift in what is *your* normal financial behavior to one that is creating wealth for your *future use.* Look around you—ever notice people of limited means driving a new BMW or Lexus? Now how do you think that happens? Are they mortgaging their futures by overspending in the present? Many believe that they can afford a car payment of "only" $479 per month for years to come. Well, guess what? They are crippling their ability to enjoy a financially secure future. The truth is that many of your peers are comfortably numb to the risk of what we will call the <u>current bank</u> and <u>future bank</u>. They are depleting their future wealth by excessive spending in the here and now. Don't get me wrong—I am not advocating that you live like a miser, saving all your money and eating frozen meals every night. What I am suggesting is that you find a balance between current spending and setting aside significant sums of money to fund a comfortable future. I want you to recognize that you will need both self-discipline and a *strategy* to achieve this result.

Think of current bank as what is in your pocket now: bank and credit union accounts, checking, savings, CD's, money markets, stocks, bonds, mutual funds, IRA's, 401(k) plans and the like.

The future bank may be thought of as the potential future value of these balances achieved through both compounding and additional contributions for the years between now and when your paychecks stop. A robust future bank will not be possible without your being willing to invest in yourself to help ensure a future of financial abundance. You may be unable to manufacture a *monthly paycheck* without a substantial future bank.

There are absolutely no guarantees concerning your future. The reason is simple: much, if not all, depends on your <u>willingness</u> to do what is necessary to secure it. I can provide effective and proven steps – but you must take them. I may be able to lead you to the door of prosperity, but you must have the courage to walk through it. No one can promise that, by reading this book, or any other, you will be financially secure. The steps you take to ensure your financial security must be taken by you and no one else. I assure you that your future financial security is not hidden within a *YouTube* video or page 67 of a monthly financial magazine.

As you read through this book, I will suggest a number of actions you can take and integrate into your financial life. You will find these in the action steps at the end of each chapter. This will take work on your part. You cannot experience meaningful long-term personal and financial growth with a series of *one-off* actions that you think will help you prepare for retirement—it must be a coordinated series of actions that bring you ever closer to your goals. If you are thinking that you can *wing it*, close this book now and buy a lottery ticket. We've got work to do, so let's do it.

CHAPTER 1

Retirement Issues You Will Face

"You can think positive all you want and you are still going to spill coffee on your new tie, get a flat tire, get cut off on the freeway, loose a big sale, get cheated, and be disappointed from time to time. Positive thinking is not about eliminating all of that from life. It is a tool to be used in more effectively coping with such events."

DAN S. KENNEDY
How to Succeed in Business by Breaking all the Rules
Dutton Books, 1997

Thinking positive will not relieve you of the necessity to save and invest for your future. Everyone I know who is financially comfortable has "paid the price" for that comfort. Unlimited spending and poor money habits did not take them to where they are today. Their constant companion was prudent decision-making, delayed gratification and prioritizing what was important to them. I also know people who are in their 50s and 60s who have accumulated very little funds or, in some cases, none at all for their retirement years. They could have prepared and done the same things required of the successful people, only they didn't do them.

If you believe you are behind in your saving and investing for retirement, or if you have not begun to save at all, you are not alone. In fact, you have plenty of company. In a March 2015 report entitled "The Continuing Retirement Savings Crisis" issued by the National Institute on Retirement Security, authors Rhee and Boivie report that 40 million working-age households in America do not own any retirement account assets. This includes both IRA's and employer-sponsored plans. Additionally, they report that 62% of working households age 55 to 64 have retirement savings equal to less than one times their annual income. How would you expect to retire with savings equal to one year's income? I encourage you to review the report in its entirety on the National Institute on Retirement Security website, http://www.nirsonline.org/.

Furthermore, the average American's income in retirement is a bit over $1,500 per month. That is approximately $18,000 annually. These numbers come from the Pension Rights Center and paint a scary picture. There will be many more people retiring with similar incomes in the not-so-distant future. I do not want you to be one of them. Walk into any retail store or restaurant and you will see many older folks working at menial tasks for near minimum wage. These people are not there of their own volition. They are there because they have no choice. If I cannot convince you to take significant steps to improve your future financial situation, you may end up with few alternatives as well.

You Do Not Want To End Up In Your Sister's Basement

Becoming aware of the potentially severe consequences if you do not make planning and investing for retirement a priority is a great first step. I doubt you would look forward to being a greeter at a big box store in your golden years. Nor would you want to work side by side with hormone-raging, pimple-faced teenagers at the local fast food joint, silly hat and all, to make ends meet. Being 70 years old and trying to figure out a computer masquerading as a cash register is not my idea of a stress-free retirement.

Most definitely, you do not want to end up in your sister's basement, or worse, your kids' basements because you had failed to plan and then ran out of money. Explaining to your future granddaughter why you live in her basement is not a conversation you will eagerly anticipate. <u>You will either have a plan for your future, or you will reluctantly be part of someone else's plans for you</u>. Which sounds more appealing? Which allows you to chart your own course? Think about the kind of future you can build for yourself. Care about it so much that you begin to build that future month-by-month and year-by-year.

Mel Robbins, in her wonderful book, *Stop Saying You're Fine: Discover a More Powerful You,* says that one-third of American men and women are dissatisfied with their lives. Mel speaks of adult malaise and the millions of adult Americans who are unhappy with their lives, look in the mirror daily and say "is this all there is?"

You don't want to be
a loser in Loserville.

RETIREMENT IS NOT CHEAP

Think how dissatisfied you might be when you are in your sixties or seventies and you have just enough money to live on but no more. Growing old in retirement is not cheap. You will need a pile of dollars set aside, and that pile is bigger than you think. It will take years to accumulate the needed funds. Now, let me compound the problem. You need to be aware that inflation is one of the most important issues that you will face in retirement. Whatever amounts of money you will need to live on, the problem is magnified when you consider the effects that inflation will have on your personal finances in retirement.

Stop and answer this question honestly: are you and your significant other prepared for the possibility of three-decade retirements with the prices of goods and services increasing, on average, between 2% and 4% each year? Your costs increase the longer you live. You are aware that everything you buy today costs more than it did 5 or 10 years ago. That's inflation!

Many of us have family members who have lived into their 90s, yet we don't believe we will live that long. According to the Social Security Administration, "about one out of every four 65-year olds today will live past age 90, and one out of every 10 will live past age 95." Advances in medical science have altered once-fatal diseases into chronic conditions, allowing people to live with diseases that were previously death sentences.

By now, you are aware that the term inflation refers to a general increase in the level of prices that you pay for goods and services over time. A 3% annual inflation rate does not seem unreasonably high until you compound it year after year. Consider this: if you need $50,000 of retirement income today you will need $65,200 in 10 years. In 20 years, you would need $87,700 to match your purchasing power of today. Now I would like you to pause here for a moment, and reflect on this question: What is your strategy to deal with this? If a blank sheet of paper comes to mind, keep reading.

CHALLENGES AWAIT YOU

Many of us are not prepared for life without a paycheck and fear that it is too late to begin saving for a future of ever-increasing expenses. The fact is that it is never too late to begin to save. Changes in your lifestyle, e.g. two less outings for expensive coffee or meals at pricey restaurants, are a good beginning. You would be amazed at how much money you might save by preparing meals at home and saving dinners out for special occasions only.

Inflation is one of many challenges waiting for you in retirement. No less scary is the issue of healthcare costs and insurance premiums. Many will no longer be covered by an employer's health insurance program and will be forced to shoulder the cost of health care premiums alone. This adds uncertainty to what your expenses might be. You may have read headlines during 2016 about the cost of some health care premiums increasing over 100%. Not to understand the importance of healthcare costs in retirement is like sticking your head in the sand and hoping you won't get sick.

An article entitled "Health Care Costs for Couples in Retirement Rise to an Estimated $260,000, Fidelity Analysis Shows" appeared August 16th, 2016, on the Fidelity Investments website. The article went on to say "paying for health care can be one of the largest expenses for people in retirement. A 65-year-old couple retiring in 2016 will need an estimated $260,000 to cover health care costs in retirement, according to Fidelity's Retiree Health Care Cost Estimate. This is a six percent increase over last year's estimate of $245,000 and the highest estimate since calculations began in 2002. The estimate applies to retirees with traditional Medicare insurance coverage and provides a general idea of the monthly expenses associated with Medicare premiums, Medicare co-payments and deductibles, and prescription drug out-of-pocket expenses."

It is beyond the scope of this book to review the intricacies of Medicare premiums, health care savings accounts and the complexity of healthcare costs. Suffice it to say that you will be challenged to save not only for retirement living expense but health care costs and insurance premiums as well. I assure you that, if you attempt to wing this without careful planning, you will most likely fail.

Before I bring this chapter to a close, here are five major risks you will face as you move ever closer to the day you retire:

- **Inflation**—many assets that you set aside for future retirement may erode in value as inflation causes increases in the future costs of most services and goods you will purchase.

- **Longevity**—So many people underestimate how long they will live and run a real risk of outliving the assets they set aside for retirement.

- **Withdrawal rate**—too high a rate of withdrawal from your investment and retirement accounts will increase the risk that you will deplete the accounts prematurely.

- **Healthcare expenses**—the increased costs of health care, rising health insurance premiums and inadequate coverage all combine to potentially cripple a retirement income plan.

- **Asset allocation**—to the extent that one owns more assets that generate fixed income and which are viewed as generally conservative in nature, such ownership may actually expose individuals to a higher risk of outliving their assets.

ACTION STEPS:

1. Take a 30-day inventory of your spending patterns and routines by carrying a small notebook and jotting down all your expenditures. Like many Americans, you may have fallen into the habit of buying snacks and fancy coffee on the run, as well as lunches and dinners in restaurants. No lecturing on my part, but I simply want you to gain an awareness of the amount of dollars running through your hands.

2. Review the last five big purchases you made. Did you buy them on credit or pay for them in full? Were they impulse buys or planned expenditures? Were they a need or a want?

3. Pull out your records and examine how much you spent on healthcare premiums, out-of-pocket expenses, co-pays and prescription drug costs in the last 12 months. If your employer paid

any part of your healthcare premiums, add those in as well. Now consider if you were responsible for 100% of the cost. How would you pay those added expenses without going into debt?

CHAPTER 2

Are You Willing To Do What Is Necessary?

"What is opportunity, and when does it knock? It never knocks. You can wait a whole lifetime, listening, hoping, and you will hear no knocking. None at all. You are opportunity, and you must knock on the door leading to your destiny."

Maxwell Maltz

A sk yourself this question: are you willing to do what is necessary to ensure that you have a comfortable retirement? You can either make excuses, or you can make progress, but you can't do both. You must have a belief that you can succeed at funding a comfortable retirement – where money will no longer be an obstacle to living the life you envision.

You know full well that if you can't convince yourself that this is doable you have a slim chance of making it happen. Your mindset is vitally important here, and we will revisit this throughout the book.

Begin a program of investing a portion of each dollar you earn for your future. Notice, I did not say a portion of some of the dollars you earn, I mean a portion of *all* of the dollars you earn. You cannot expect to be successful in this if you save what is left over at month's end. The more awareness I can bring to bear in these words, the better; hopefully, I will move you to take action. You must begin paying yourself first before you pay credit card bills, a utility bill or a car loan. You pay yourself with each dollar you earn.

LEARN TO LIVE ON LESS THAN YOU EARN

Look at it this way: do you believe that you can be comfortable and have sufficient funds in retirement if you don't make saving and investing for retirement a priority? If you do, what will be the source of the money? Will Uncle Louie or Aunt Sophie leave you a bundle in their will? Will you win big in a lottery? Will the U.S.

Government inform you that you have overpaid your taxes for 35 years and send you a check for $350,000? The answer to all of these musings is *DOUBTFUL*. It is highly unlikely that any of these scenarios will come to pass. Therefore, what *you must do* is plan and take action.

Imagine if you started to invest funds from paychecks starting with your very first real job. Suppose you placed three cents of each dollar earned in your very own financial fortress account that compounded for decades. You learned how to survive on 97 cents of each dollar earned, 96 cents, 95 cents and so on. You invested in tax-advantaged retirement accounts such as a 401(k) or IRA account. You invested those funds for capital growth, knowing they would have decades to grow. Over time, you learn how to live on 90 cents, and finally 85 cents of each dollar you earned. The potential growth over decades is staggering. What you have at work here is the time value of money!

THE POWER OF TIME AND COMPOUNDING

Read on and I will let you in on some really interesting financial math.

> *The truth is that we create our own opportunities by the way we think, by the decisions we make and by the peer groups with whom we spend our time.*

Assume you are 40 years old and you place $5,500 in a Roth IRA compounding annually at 8%. Let us further assume you will retire at age 65. You have a 25-year period of time for the funds to grow and compound. Guess how much your initial investment of $5,500 will be worth at the end of this 25-year period? The amount is $37,666.*

Now, imagine for a moment that you are funding the Roth IRA every single year. Let us use the example above, and add in that you are now placing $5,500 a year in the same investment and that you are funding it monthly, to the tune of $458.33 per month. That's a little more than $15 per day. That does not seem unreasonable, does it? In case you are

---

* The examples provided are hypothetical and have been included for illustrative purposes only. These examples are not intended to reflect the actual performance of any particular security. Future investment performance cannot be guaranteed and investment yields will fluctuate with market conditions.

EUREKA!
Time and compounding is the answer!

wondering, in 25 years, you would have a total of $439,746.

The power of time and compounding is nothing short of remarkable. Now, you may have more or less than 25 years to compound your money, but there are still strategies that you can use to put time and compounding on your side. Now, assume for just a moment that this Roth IRA strategy is just one part of your overall strategy. I hope you can see the potential benefits of just one strategy. Just imagine if you were to implement a number of changes, not just one!

You may have limited resources, but it is within all of us to be resourceful. This book is a resource (so don't say you have no resources!). I have failed plenty of times at many things. That does not mean I gave up and threw in the towel. From time to time I blamed a lack of resources. I told myself that I did not have the time, the money, the knowledge or the help I needed, and that was why I failed. A more likely reason, although I did not want to admit it, was that I lacked resourcefulness. My problem was that I suffered from one-dimensional thinking. When I had no money I sat on my couch and blamed myself for not having opportunities.

> *If you'd like a free report on*
> *"The 12 Keys to Successful Retirement Planning*
> *Your Parents Didn't Teach You", go to*
> <u>www.RodgeronRetirement.com</u> *and enter your*
> *name and e-mail address in the box.*

A WHOPPING $600

When I was younger and scrounging for dimes and quarters in my sofa, I found it much easier to blame others, to blame events or even to blame my employer or the economy. For a while, I blamed the Democrats, and then I decided it was the Republicans' fault. I was an equal opportunity blamer! The last person in the world I wanted to blame was myself. When I started saving for my own retirement, I put a whopping $600 in an IRA account. That's $11.53 per week or $1.65 per day. I would challenge you to find a cup of coffee for that amount!

Jim Rohn, one of America's foremost business philosophers, was quoted as saying that you can't blame the only stuff with which you have to work. Seed and soil and sunshine and rain—that's all there is. He told me to grow up and fix the blame where it belongs—on myself. Jim said that I was not going to be able to change anything external, but I could change myself. He said *I had to work harder on myself than I do on my job.* Those words resonated with me and I hope they resonate with you as well.

I decided that my life could be financially successful if I really worked at it. Now I ask you, have you ever run into a poor success? Of course not! I want you to be preparing for a financially abundant retirement, with a

> *Don't be afraid to fail. Everyone I know who is very successful has frequently failed. They failed and failed until they succeeded.*

rock solid balance sheet. For additional lessons on this, I suggest you read my book Fire Your Retirement Planner: You! I think you will find it to be a helpful tool with plenty of useful lessons. The book is available on my website: www.RodgeronRetirement.com or on Amazon.

Here's the key: you must develop a willingness to try, and fail, and try again until you succeed. Very few people succeed at anything their first time around. Know any good drivers who failed their first driving test? Know any doctors that barely graduated from medical school? Know any lawyers who failed the bar exam the first or second time? We have all failed at something. The lack of failure is often a sign of the lack of trying new things.

Face it: genius is not the norm in America or anywhere in the world. You must be willing to develop a program of savings and investing, and to guard against depleting the funds for a new car, a vacation, a new bedroom set or dining room table. You must learn to balance between what you want to buy now, and what you need to save for in the future. Know this: you will stumble, you will fall, and you will utterly fail from time to time. It is up to you to get up off the floor and start again, and this time, do it smarter. Tony Robbins taught me that I must keep my goals in mind, see what is working and adjust my course as I go.

ACTION STEPS:

1. Write down five ways that you can cut back on your monthly spending and circle three of them that you can eliminate in the next 30 days. Great start; now make it real.

2. Take an inventory of your assets (what you own) and your liabilities (what you owe). Review and study them. If I woke you up out of a dead sleep, I want you to rattle them off without hesitation.

3. Learn the difference between saving and investing. Pick up a great book on the subject: The Elements of Investing: Easy Lessons for Every Investor, Wiley, 2nd edition, 2013, by Burton G. Malkiel and Charles Ellis. Read it twice!

CHAPTER 3

Visualize Your Ideal Retirement

"Whatever you want to see in your life that's not there now is about growth. Growth is at the root of everything that gives us a feeling of accomplishment, satisfaction, meaning, and progress."

DAN SULLIVAN & CATHERINE NOMURA

The Laws of Lifetime Growth

Berrett-Koehler Publishers, 2006

L et's talk about attitude. Ever try to have a positive experience with a lousy attitude? As you begin to consider your future retirement, it would help if you frame it as a positive experience and not the end of the productive period of your life. The transition from "working for a living" to "enjoying the rest of your life" will require a change of mindset and a fair amount of soul searching. I have known many people who have not made the transition well.

What would your calendar look like and what would you want to accomplish when you have control of each 24-hour day? How will your life change when you no longer have to be "somewhere" from nine to five? Despite what some people might say, you will most likely not play golf or tennis seven days a week. Create a balance of activities that include long overdue enjoyments, learning and community service, as well as physical activities to keep you healthy.

Shortly after I graduated from college in upstate New York, some friends made plans to backpack through Europe, living on the cheap in youth hostels and traveling with the Eurail Pass. They were able to spend four months abroad and create lifelong memories in a dozen countries for a ridiculously small amount of money. I have always regretted not joining them on their adventure. Thirty-nine years later, the first item on my unfinished business list is to spend a month and hop from one European country to another, staying in fine hotels instead of youth hostels. Decades of saving have now made such travel within reach. Additionally, I will have the wonderful company of my wife Reena so I will not be country hopping alone. Although neither Reena nor I have any family in Europe, I'm certain we can find enough points of interest to keep us happily busy for 30 days.

KEEP YOUR MIND AND BODY ENGAGED

You may find yourself more involved with family than in previous years. Additional free time provides more opportunity to visit family members who don't live nearby. It is never too early to focus on what you want to do with your life after your primary career ends. Hopefully, the remainder of your life will prove to be long and healthy, and you will need important activities to keep yourself engaged. It might be a useful exercise for you to jot down all the things you have wanted to do in your life but have not yet done. Some call it their bucket list; others refer to it as their unfinished business. Whatever you call it, write it down and make the list. It may prove to be some of the most important thoughts you have committed to paper.

Pretend that you are retiring next month. Visualize your calendar of activities. What would you do on Monday, Tuesday, and Wednesday? What is your reason for getting out of bed? Will you be productive tending to your garden, or will you stare into space wondering what to do? Let me say this again: clarity is essential. People have a very hard time envisioning their future. Now, what do *you* envision? What does it mean to you? What is your reason for getting out of bed? You can't hit a target you can't see. Here are some activities to get your brain started thinking on the right path:

- Softball
- Tennis
- Bowling
- Cycling
- Hiking
- Fishing
- Boating
- Teaching
- Volunteering
- Back to school
- Chess
- Coaching
- Photography
- Coin collecting
- Quilting
- Cooking
- Woodworking
- Crafts
- Yoga
- Weightlifting
- Tai Chi
- Fencing

- Feldenkreis
- Basketball
- Ping-Pong
- Stamp collecting
- Billiards
- Gardening
- Swimming
- Massage
- Painting

- Scrapbooking
- Sculpting
- Writing
- Dance
- Archery
- Water aerobics
- Theatre
- Opera
- Singing

I have listed many activities that you can enjoy with your spouse or significant other at a reasonable cost, or at no cost at all. Many of these will keep you active and possibly lead to a longer and healthier life.

Heck, you might buy or adopt a dog and spend hours each day hiking around the neighborhood. When you retire, you know that many activities will cost money, but many will not. Figure out what you like to do and create plans with a small team of advisors and invest your assets accordingly. If you want to participate in scuba trips to the Cayman Islands, then perhaps you might invest more for growth and recognize a need to step up your savings and investment programs.

ACTION STEPS:

1. List at least five activities you enjoy that cost little or no money.

2. Think of three physical activities that you enjoy and three activities that require you to concentrate and use your brain.

3. Use your imagination – sketch out a month full of activity and convince yourself that it could be a normal month of your life.

CHAPTER 4

Hold Yourself Accountable

"The tragedy of life doesn't lie in not reaching your goal. The tragedy lies in having no goal to reach."

BENJAMIN E. MAYES

I'm sorry to be the one to tell you this, but if you screw up, there is no one but yourself to blame. There is an old line, "If not me, then who?" It's a good question. You must depend upon yourself to build up your retirement nest egg. Rarely will you be able to point to someone else and say, "It's your fault I have no money for retirement!"

What is required is an accurate assessment of where you are now and where you wish to be financially in the future, and measuring the gap that exists between those two points. We would all like to spend the money we earn on improving our current lifestyle. A larger home, a new car or granite countertops in the kitchen are some items that may be on your personal wish list. The reality is that, with limited resources, you need to prioritize what is most important.

> *You choose your level of wealth by the choices you make about money.*

At a recent gathering, I observed two couples, both with new cell phones in hand, comparing the cuteness of their emojis. For those readers who are at a loss to understand the last sentence, let me explain. Emojis are those cute little symbols and images that people attach to text messages and E-mails. They spent the better part of 30 minutes showing each other how to download apps that contain additional images so that they can send even more cute messages. I couldn't help but wonder why they felt this was an important subject of discussion.

I blew a lot of money on this phone,
but the apps are so cool!!
I can contribute to my IRA next year.

A Cool Phone Versus an IRA Contribution

I overheard how one had just purchased her new phone at a big box electronic store and "only pays" $35.42 per month. She sheepishly admitted that the charges continued for 24 months, and the choice was between funding her IRA and buying the phone. She related that she could put money in the IRA next year instead. Now, I don't pretend to be a math whiz, but the last time I multiplied $35.42 by 24, I arrived at slightly more than $850. That is $850 for a new phone so that she could send cute text messages and pictures featuring the latest emojis. Evidently, her old phone was not up to the task. I couldn't help but wonder what her IRA statement looked like!

Too bad there is no app to tell her that maintaining this kind of spending pattern on frivolous items will likely severely damage any hope of a financially secure retirement. Financial discipline is needed to ensure we do not make poor financial decisions. One of the most important aspects of investing for a secure future retirement is to invest early. This means that the more time funds are left to grow and compound, the better. The time value of money is vitally important. By delaying investments in favor of spending on the here and now, less money is available to grow for the future.

Here is a compelling example of the true power of deciding to save early.

Barbara decides to begin saving for retirement at age 20. She arranges her finances so that she saves $3,000 annually for the next 10 years. Barbara is earning 8% per year on her investments. She stops investing after 10 years at age 30.

Jonathan is very different from Barbara. He loves purchasing new things and never tires of buying the latest gadget. He decides to delay saving for retirement until he is age 30. Like Barbara, he invests $3,000 per year. However, he does this for 30 years. He is also earning an 8% return. At the end of 30 years, Jonathan stops contributing.*

At age 60, Barbara's retirement account balance is approximately $472,000. Remember, she invested only $30,000 and then stopped. Meanwhile, Jonathan's retirement account balance grew to roughly $367,000 after investing $90,000 over 30 years. As

---

* The examples provided are hypothetical and have been included for illustrative purposes only. These examples are not intended to reflect the actual performance of any particular security. Future investment performance cannot be guaranteed and investment yields will fluctuate with market conditions.

you see, time matters and so does your mindset. Would you rather emulate Barbara or Jonathan as a retirement investor? Who has taken greater personal responsibility for their future? Barbara invested one-third of what Jonathan invested, yet ended up with more than $100,000 additional dollars.

THE TIME TO BEGIN BUILDING
FUTURE WEALTH IS NOW

Unfortunately, way too many people approaching retirement are ill- prepared. If you do not prepare for your own retirement, do not expect assistance from the government, either in terms of preparation or a financial "bail out." In all probability, they will provide you with a Social Security check, but that's about it. You won't live high on the hog on a government check. It is a much better idea to do what you can, when you can, to ensure a comfortable retirement. The point is that the sooner you begin to take planning seriously, the more alternatives and options will be available to you. You will lose a lot of flexibility years from now. There are many ways you can begin to build a secure future, and the time to begin building future wealth is now.

Here is a list of some of the most common types of retirement plans you may have available to you:

- Traditional IRA
- Roth IRA
- 401(k) plan
- Roth 401(k) plan
- Simple IRA
- SEP IRA
- 403(b) plan
- Profit sharing plan
- Money purchase plan

A 401(k) or 403(b) plan, if offered by your employer, might be an excellent place to begin. I have seen first-rate plans with very attractive features, and also plans that offer a more basic bare-bones approach. Whatever type of employer-sponsored retirement plan you are offered, here are some words of advice. Learn about the plan and how it can benefit you. You may be given a brochure or a website to review the particulars of the plan. I suggest you allocate sufficient time to study it, become familiar with how it works and how you can take maximum advantage of it. These resources often show examples of how you may wish to allocate plan balances, along with different contribution levels and benefits such as matching employer contributions.

If you have questions, ask the appropriate human resources or benefits person in your company. Do not let temporary confusion keep you from making an informed decision. Put your ego aside and do not be embarrassed to ask questions and say you do not understand something. The choice of whether you participate, and your level of participation in an employer plan, will have far-reaching consequences for your future finances. If you have someone you trust to help you make more informed decisions, by all means, consult him or her.**

Participating in an employer-sponsored retirement plan is but one of many strategies you might employ. As private employers have minimized the use of defined

---

** Matching contributions from your employer may be subject to a vesting schedule. Please review your plan documents or consult with your financial advisor for more information.

benefit pension plans in favor of defined contribution, or 401(k) plans, the onus for retirement savings has shifted in large part from the employer to the employee.

Relatively few employers will accept the responsibility of providing retirement income until death. What this means, very simply, is that you cannot ignore the importance of actively and continuously saving and investing for the day your paychecks stop. To the extent possible, you will also want to contribute to your own IRA or Individual Retirement Account. As this may be outside your comfort zone, why not enlist the help of a partner to keep you on track?

WHEN YOU LEARNED TO SWIM

Consider the idea of a "buddy system." You remember when you learned to swim, you would be assigned a "buddy" who would look out for you and make sure you didn't get into trouble or drown? Well, let's extend this concept a bit. Why not arrange with a friend to *check in* periodically, say, every Friday afternoon? Try spending 20 minutes on the phone so you can relate all the things you did right and all the things you screwed up, for the past week. Share with him or her how much of your "to do" list you actually got done. Be sure to tell your buddy how you plan to correct your mistakes and improve your performance next week.

> *"Throughout my life, I have put my goals down in writing, enlisting people to help me achieve them. I make quarterly reports to what I call the board of directors of my life: 5 people who hold me accountable to my goals. Every year I review my goals and share them in detail. Then, quarterly, I look at what went right and what went wrong, preparing for the annual report."*
>
> **JACK DALY**
> Hyper Sales Growth
> Advantage Media Group, 2014

Your accountability buddy will also have the opportunity for you to be their sounding board as well. You will be helping each other. The main idea here is to improve your financial behavior week after week, month after month. Most likely you will not want to share with your buddy that you spent $38 on coffee drinks for the week. Imagine your buddy calling you out on your coffee spending, lecturing you that, if you placed $150 monthly in an account left to compound at 6% annually for the next 12 years, you would have a little more than $30,000 to add to your wealth. You might respond with "Where did you come up with $150 per month?" Your buddy will clue you in that that's the amount of money you are spending each month on coffee! If you have someone with whom you have to check in, you are more likely to stick to your plan, rather than have to explain that you fell flat on your face! This is the nature of accountability and is all about personal responsibility. *If it's to be, it's up to me* sums it up quite well. Unfortunately, mom and dad are not here to make sure you get this done. Taking responsibility means continuously working to build your retirement savings balances so that you will have the freedom of choosing your desired retirement lifestyle, whatever that lifestyle may be. In the action steps that follow, I will ask you to see what your projected Social Security income *might* be at retirement. Prepare to be shocked.***

*** The examples provided are hypothetical and have been included for illustrative purposes only. These examples are not intended to reflect the actual performance of any particular security. Future investment performance cannot be guaranteed and investment yields will fluctuate with market conditions.

If you would like the transcript of Rodger's insightful In Depth TV interview with Dr. George Flinn, please send your request to Info@RodgeronRetirement.com *and we will e-mail you the full transcript.*

ACTION STEPS:

1. Request your Social Security annual statement. The report contains a record of your earnings and projections of your retirement income provided by the government. Visit the Social Security Administration website at SSA.GOV and search for *My Social Security*.

2. Determine what your annual income gap is in retirement— i.e., the gap between what Social Security might provide and the amount of annual retirement income you would like. For example, suppose Social Security will provide

$24,000 per year of the $53,000 you desire. You have a gap of $29,000 annually. Congratulations! Now write it down and make it real. You cannot deal with a problem that's a "maybe" and might not actually exist.

3. Now that the problem just became real for you, *determine if and how you can solve it yourself.* Don't work yourself to death; recognize it is time to bring in some help.

CHAPTER 5

---

*Don't Go It Alone;
Assemble a Team*

W hile attending a professional conference in Texas, I sat listening to the keynote address presented by football legend Emmitt Smith. He is considered by many to be one of the greatest running backs in NFL history. From All-American at the University of Florida to 15 seasons in the NFL, he managed to break Walter Peyton's record as the NFL's all-time rushing leader. As I sat there, I thought to myself that this fellow knows a bit about determination, focus, and success. I grabbed a sharp pencil and began to take notes.

He spoke about adversity and having to figure out a way to overcome it. He said, "*It's time to change. Do not let challenges paralyze you.*" He recommended we ask for assistance from others, and stop being stubborn and thinking that we can do everything by ourselves.

He said that it is important to surround yourself in life with people who can help you. You will spend too much time trying to accomplish things if you try to do it all by yourself. He said do not be afraid to ask for help. He told us that when he decided to quit football, he turned to others for guidance, advice, and strategy. He recognized that as good as he was in A, that success did not necessarily translate to B. At this point, perhaps you are thinking of contacting him to assist you in your own retirement planning. Quite frankly, I wouldn't blame you!

WHO HAS YOUR BACK?

So I ask you, whom do you have in your life that makes sure you are prudently investing for the future? Who is it that determines if you are taking too much risk or not enough risk? Is there someone whose job it is to make sure you are invested properly? Is there someone who makes certain that you have the proper amount of life, disability, and home insurance? Is there someone, anyone, who is concerned that you get these decisions right and that you do not expose yourself and your family to unnecessary risks? In other words, *who has your back*?

Who makes sure you do not do something dumb or foolish? You see, the idea of preparing for retirement has become more complex than just looking forward to a monthly Social Security check in the mailbox and sitting on the front porch. Relaxing and waiting for the mailman, check in hand, might have been fine for grandpa, but you are a different story.

Our financial lives have become much more complicated than during our grandparents' time. Years ago, families dealt with a bank for savings and mortgages, an insurance company for all types of insurance, a lawyer for a will and a stockbroker for stocks and bonds. Your grandparents' retirement income was derived primarily from Social Security payments. Add to that, their life expectancies were quite a bit shorter than today.

Now we have IRA's and Roth IRA's, 401(k) and 403(b) plans, Simple IRA's and more. Americans are retiring earlier and living longer. It is not uncommon to imagine that you or your spouse may enjoy a joint 30-year retirement. That means that the last of you might pass 30 years after you stopped working. Try tackling all this yourself and you're liable to end up with a massive headache and poor results. The reason is that, as good as you are at your job, whatever that might be, this important area of your life is something that you simply are not trained for and you do not possess the necessary expertise to get it right.

Listen To Tom

In his 2001 book, *The Millionaire Mind*, author Thomas J. Stanley said: "There is a strong positive correlation between finding good advisors and wealth accumulation, because having good advice reduces the risk involved in financial, career, and even personal decisions."

That said, I want to open your eyes to how ill prepared many adults are for a financially secure retirement. They view Social Security as their primary source of income.

In a November 14th, 2016, *Time Magazine* article entitled "The Next President's Financial Imperative:

Fixing Social Security," the authors stated that "Today, some 60% of Americans age 65 or older rely on Social Security for 50% or more of their family income—the average payment is a modest $1300 a month. For some 33% of families, the benefit makes up 90% to 100% of their income."

Sailing into retirement without a well-thought-out plan is as knuckleheaded as taking a boat ride with your idiot nephew with no life preservers. Many make misguided decisions on when to begin receiving retirement benefits. Rarely is it a wise decision to rely on advice from Social Security personnel as to when you should begin receiving retirement benefits. That is not their function. The intelligent thing to do is to have your own small team of advisors – your CFP® and CPA to help guide you to make the best decisions possible. Yes, it will cost money, but I view it as money well spent.

In a *Reuters* article published on September 22nd, 2016, the author, Mark Miller, discussed how irregularities at the Social Security Administration actually had claims specialists making personal recommendations to seniors signing up for benefits that were forbidden under agency guidelines. Miller went on to say that a report by the General Accounting Office—the investigative arm of Congress—was prepared at the behest of the U.S. Senate Special Committee on Aging to review this issue.

While the Social Security Administration does a tremendous job of providing income to tens of millions of Americans, I doubt that the job description of their claims specialists is to provide individualized personal financial planning advice. That is the job of a trained retirement professional.

THE KEY TO ACHIEVING THE OUTCOME YOU WANT

During my 30-plus years as a professional financial advisor focusing on retirement issues, I have witnessed many wonderful retirement outcomes and many that ended poorly. Seeking help *may be* the key to your achieving the outcome you want. I believe you should assemble a small team to guide and assist you that includes the following:

- CERTIFIED FINANCIAL PLANNER™

- A CPA or accountant
- An independent insurance agent
- A mentor

Your accountability buddy stands apart from the team we will talk about now. The relationship with your buddy will tend to be more intimate. This is a person who can, and will, call you out when you mess up. Now, let's spend some time to discuss who makes up your team.

First is your retirement planning professional. He or she is the quarterback of your team. This individual has completed a comprehensive curriculum of study that includes personal financial planning techniques and strategies, taxation, investments, retirement and estate planning. This is the individual who can help you plan your investment strategy.

Next is your CPA or Certified Public Accountant. He or she will be responsible for your tax planning as well as assisting you in filing your annual federal and state tax returns, assisting with quarterly tax payments, if necessary, and a wide variety of other tax issues. I have never met a dumb accountant. Leverage your relationship with this person and turn to them for advice and referrals to other professionals. Many individuals opt for online services that allow them to submit their tax returns inexpensively. This should not take the place of competent personalized tax planning.

Your independent insurance professional will assist you in choosing the right type of insurance coverage for your particular situation. I strongly recommend that you only deal with an independent agent. We all know the story of the fellow who wanders onto a Ford lot and may be a perfect candidate for a Toyota. However, the odds are that he will be sold a Ford. An independent agent may be able to look at many products from different providers to determine which are best for you, your needs and your budget. They will not be limited to the products of one company.

Your mentor should be someone you know and trust who is very successful in his or her own career. This may be a family friend or a highly accomplished colleague in your industry. This is an additional individual to whom you can turn for trusted advice to keep you on the right track and to help you make sound and prudent decisions. It would not hurt if this person were someone who is comfortable with financial matters and possesses sound judgment, and it might be a good idea if this person is a bit older than you with more experience.

Jim Rohn would say, "The greatest reward in becoming a millionaire is not the amount of money that you earn. It is the kind of person that you have to become to become a millionaire in the first place." You want to be able to engage in important conversations with such a person. Think of what you can learn from them!

THE DECISIONS ARE YOURS TO MAKE

I think some words of caution would be helpful here. First, all of the individuals discussed above are there to assist you in creating a future of financial abundance. They are *not* there to do your thinking for you. In each and every circumstance, these individuals are there to have a collaborative relationship with you. You *cannot* abdicate thinking to someone else. Yes, they might possess the technical expertise you need to make good decisions, but, in the final analysis, the decisions are yours to make. Success or failure is still in your hands.

You cannot hire someone to do pushups for you. There is a big difference between receiving good advice and recommendations and actually being the kind of person who listens and, after contemplation, implements those recommendations.

Second, do not confuse technology with prudent advice. The apps on our phones can connect us to stock exchanges, banks, and insurance companies. We can take a picture of a check and make a deposit without ever going to the bank or file an insurance claim and transmit pictures of our car accidents. You can trade stocks while walking down the street. Even though we can do all of these things, we may still lack the wisdom to make sure we are doing the right things for our families. Just because you can do something fast or efficiently does not mean you are being effective.

Although I can purchase a couple hundred shares of stock on my phone in seconds, this does not mean it's a good idea or a sound investment. *Technology does not create sound judgment.*

Technology will not stop you from doing something stupid. That is the job of a mentor or an advisor. I hope you know to whom to turn when you need advice or guidance. When it comes to growing your wealth for retirement, seek the assistance of trained professionals *and* a mentor.

ACTION STEPS:

1. Ask three colleagues or friends if they work with a CERTIFIED FINANCIAL PLAN-NER™, and ask for a referral. If none work with a planner, ask three more and repeat as many times as is necessary.

2. Interview a minimum of three professionals to determine if they have experience working with people similar to you and that you share a comfortable chemistry.

3. Repeat this same exercise to find a CPA and an independent insurance agent. Do not rush this process. Take the time to do it right.

RODGER ON RETIREMENT
SPECIAL REPORT
EIGHT CONTROL FACTORS THAT
DETERMINE RETIREMENT SUCCESS

When the day comes for you to retire and you receive your last paycheck, what is your plan to create an income that will sustain your lifestyle? This special report will discuss and review eight Control Factors that may well determine if you will ever be able to enjoy a lifestyle-sustaining income in retirement.

Visit RodgeronRetirtement.com/shop

CHAPTER 6

Set Higher Goals

"You're the average of the 5 people you spend the most time with."

JIM ROHN

O K, who do you spend the most time with? Now think for a minute. Do these five close friends save and invest for their future; do they read books that will fill gaps in their knowledge; do you brainstorm and challenge each other? Or perhaps they never miss an opportunity for happy hour and entertainment? If their average bank balance is $18,000, odds are your balance is not far from theirs. You see, a closely-knit group of friends often pick up each other's habits. If they are in debt, have you emulated their behavior? If you are going to model the habits of others, make certain they are good habits. With that said, let's talk a bit about debt, specifically credit card debt.

Hopefully, you are not one of the tens of millions of Americans who have become numb to the amount of debt you have accumulated. I have witnessed how debt can derail even the most ambitious plans people may have for a financially successful retirement.

In the early 80s, I got myself into trouble with credit card debt. Reflecting back now, it was not a great deal of money, but at the time it was a great deal to me. I secured a MasterCard and Visa from two local banks. Here I was with four credit cards, each with a $700 credit limit. The average interest rate on my credit cards at the time was about 17%. I quickly managed to get myself into trouble, paying off a monthly minimum by taking a cash advance from one of the other cards. This strategy worked for a very short time and then blew up in my face. You see, I was buying things I could not afford and going deeper and deeper into debt. But I wasn't alone; you see, all my friends were in credit card debt also. In fact, we would compare notes on how much we owed and the amounts of our minimum monthly payments.

A shot in the butt or pills will not cure you of poor retirement investing habits.

How many people do you know that are comfortably numb with their credit card debt? Might you be one of *them*? Not sure what I meant by that? Does any of the following seem familiar?

- I've had so much credit card debt for so long that I just accept it as a fact of life and try not to think about it anymore.

- I have tried to reduce my debt year after year and nothing works.

- Everyone I know has a boatload of debt and I'm no different.

- My sister told me to cut up my credit cards, but I could never do that! I use them too much.

- I don't know—two cards just don't seem like enough. My friends each have five or six.

WHITTLE DOWN YOUR DEBT

If these statements are familiar to you, you are not alone; in fact, you are in the company of many others. Millions of your peers from California to Indiana to Maine share the same predicaments. Let me share with you four ideas to help you whittle down your debt and keep more of your money.

1. Identify the credit card with the highest interest rate and STOP using it! Call the bank and ask if they can lower the rate of interest. In fact, call every bank with which you do business and ask *all* of them to lower their rates. It never hurts to ask and you may be surprised when they say yes. If the clerk who answers the phone does not have the authority to lower your rate, ask to speak with a supervisor. Remind them you are a long-time client and you're thinking about transferring your balances to another bank if they do not lower your rate. Now is not the time to be timid—ask. Regardless of their offer, respond with the following: "Is that the best you can do?" Then be silent and wait. You may be offered an even lower rate.

2. The card that you want to pay off first is the one costing you the most money—that would be the one with the highest interest rate. After all, why would you pay down a loan at 7% while ignoring the loan at 15%? Answer: you wouldn't! That interest is costing you valuable dollars each

month; pay off the highest one first, then cut that card to pieces and bury it in your backyard. OK, that's not environmentally friendly. Maybe just have a nice, short ceremony and toss the pieces in the garbage. Then celebrate the fact that you have just removed the heaviest monkey from your back. Now go and repeat the process with the credit card with the second highest interest rate, then the third. Keep that scissor handy as you want to cut up all those extra cards you will no longer need.

3. Work on your psychology. How have you locked yourself into this pattern of spending? Do you spend money to celebrate? Do you spend money when you are down or bored? Take out a pencil and write down three ways you can lower your spending. Now try implementing them. Perhaps you can cook more meals at home instead of eating out several times per week. Maybe one trip to the mall each month instead of every Saturday. Be creative and figure out how *you* can cut expenses. I know—everyone hates budgeting

and you are probably no different. That doesn't mean that you can't be imaginative and figure out ways to decrease your spending.

4.   Empty out your wallet—you heard me, empty it. You do not need to carry around seven or eight credit cards every time you leave the house. Lock away all but one or two—one to use and one as a backup. If you ever want to pay down your debt and, yes, even be debt free, you will have to change the way you think about money. It is hard to get ahead financially while being shackled with debt that never seems to go away.

Years ago, I attended a Tony Robbins event where he spoke of *raising your standards.* He taught us that we need to turn our *shoulds* into *musts.* Yes, you **should** begin saving more money for retirement.

But what you really should be thinking is I **must** increase my savings for retirement! When you re-characterize something that you might do, something that you can do or something that you ought to do into an absolute must do, your thinking changes. This takes self-discipline. Your priorities change. It is a re-ordering of what is most significant to the top of your list from the bottom. Saving and investing for the future becomes an absolute must. If that becomes your governing principle, you likely will not spend $32 a week on expensive coffee.

As you raise the bar on both your financial habits as well as your financial education, be mindful of the following example. Howard Schultz of Starbucks fame became a billionaire by sticking to certain principles and focusing on what was important to achieving his goals. Like other great leaders, he believes in building a team around him with capabilities that complement his own skills. I would doubt that he would hire a first-year accountant to be his CFO. He would want someone with tens of thousands of hours of experience.

BE MINDFUL WHO TEACHES YOU ABOUT MONEY

Be mindful of from where and from whom you get your education. For example, I can write about these subjects as I have been a financial advisor for over 32 years and managed large sums of money for families preparing for their retirements. Had I graduated from college with an automotive engineering degree, I would not be qualified to teach wealth building in preparation for your retirement. Then again, maybe I could redesign your car so that it would reach 200 miles per hour!

Here is something for you to think about: although it may be a great idea to take a personal finance course at the local community college to expand your knowledge, I want to caution you about something. Dan Kennedy, who wrote extensively about "Renegade Millionaire Entrepreneurs," often warns of learning about wealth from sources that do not possess wealth. Your instructor may, in fact, be earning $52,000 per year teaching personal finance and have a savings account with a $12,000 balance. This is not the source from which I would choose to learn about wealth.

You would not go to an amateur welder to learn to weld. I would want to learn about wealth from wealthy sources that have achieved their own wealth and are happy and willing to teach others. While we would all like to learn about success and wealth building for our retirement from the Starbucks CEO, I would settle for a lesson by a *from-scratch* millionaire, i.e., an entrepreneur who has figured it out and become very successful in his or her line of work. You want to learn from someone who has *been there and done that.* In short, you want to take lessons from someone who has achieved a measure of wealth and success.

ACTION STEPS:

1. Working with your financial professionals, determine what is a reasonable goal for your monthly income in retirement and work with them to create a plan to achieve it.

2. Make a list of 12 financially successful people and figure out a way that you can interact with them and spend time with them to learn and soak up their knowledge.

3. Review your wealth and retirement plans weekly until you memorize them; once memorized, review them every three weeks.

CHAPTER 7

Get Started Now

"What you're seeking is self-determination and there is no room for timidity. In other words, more control of your future. This is about you making the decisions that will govern, define and ultimately weave the tapestry of your life. With greater wealth, come more choices and options on how you will live your life, the extent of material help to your children and grandchildren, and whether you may be able to leave a legacy to others. People do not decide their futures, they decide their habits and their habits decide their futures."

F. MATTHIAS ALEXANDER

You do not need to reinvent the wheel. There are a number of simple actions you can take that will increase your chances for a successful outcome. Here are five actions you can begin to incorporate into your life:

1. Are you eligible for a **Roth IRA**? Does the idea of tax-free retirement income interest you? There are strict eligibility rules that apply to the Roth IRA. According to the IRS, if you are married, filing your taxes jointly, and your *modified adjusted gross income* (MAGI) is less than $186,000 for 2017, you can contribute $5,500 to a Roth IRA ($6,500 if you are over age 50). If your income is between $186,000 and $196,000, you can contribute a reduced amount. If you are single and your MAGI is below $118,000, you are eligible to make a full contribution. If your income is between $118,000 and $133,000, you may make a reduced contribution.

2. You would be shocked to learn how many Americans are unknowingly declining offers of free retirement contributions from their employers. Many employers offer to contribute funds to your 401(k) or 403(b) plans in addition to the funds that you contribute. These are commonly referred to as **matching funds** or matching contributions. For example, if you contribute 5%

of your salary to your retirement plan offered by your employer, they agree to match your 5% with their own money. To be clear, if you contribute $250, your employer would match it with a $250 contribution. That is a 100% return before the funds are even invested!

3. Create a **financial fortress**. I define this as a long-term investment account where you make deposits but absolutely no withdrawals. This is the account that you will use to grow your wealth over decades. The idea here is to continually invest in assets that have the opportunity to grow over time. Do not think short term here. Find any excuse to make a deposit to this account. You stayed away from Starbucks for a week. Great. Now deposit $30 into your account. You got a pay increase? Congratulations! Now place one-third of the increase in your paycheck in the account every time you get paid. Are you expecting a refund from filing your taxes? Take one-third to one-half of the refund check and deposit it into your financial

fortress. You get the hang of it—take a third to a half and place it into your fortress.

You never use this account to buy things made of shiny plastic and metal. This is your long-term wealth account, so treat it with respect. Speak with an investment professional and identify long-term growth investments that are suitable for you. Do not use this account to speculate or to trade stocks. With that caution in mind, let me emphasize that you do want to speak with your financial planner about how best to position your assets for growth over time.

THERE IS NO MAGIC FORMULA

Understand that your investments will not grow over each and every time period—i.e., each day, each week, each month, etc. Even the best investments lose value some of the time. It is important not to panic when markets turn volatile. I urge you to speak with your team and to gain a solid understanding of investment basics. With greater understanding comes greater confidence.

For example, if my objective were to retire in 17

years, that equates to 204 months. I would not be overly worried if my investment balances were down in month 13, 47 or 68. After all, I am still contributing to these accounts month after month and, on balance, I would rather purchase assets or shares that have been marked down in price rather than more expensive shares that have been marked up in price.

I recall a mentor years ago who recommended a near 100% allocation to a diversified common stock portfolio to fund his retirement. His reasoning was that, based on historical market returns, he was willing to accept a high degree of uncertainty now in return for his invested dollars potentially growing at higher rates of return over time.

Many times, a retirement investor's worst enemy is his or her own behavior. Consider that for the 30-year period that ended on December 31, 2015, the average annual return of the Standard and Poor's (S&P™)* index was 10.35%, while the average return of equity investors

---

* The Standard and Poor's 500 Index is an unmanaged index of approximately 500 widely held us securities chosen for market size, liquidity and industry group representation. S&P500 is a registered trademark of the McGraw-Hill Company.

during the same time period was 3.66%**. The most reasonable explanation for this is poor investor behavior. By this, I mean that the average investor actually underperformed the S&P™ due to his or her behavior of moving in and out of equity investments due to fear, greed, poor advice or other reasons. In order to attain the higher return, all the investor had to do was leave his or her investment alone—in other words.... do nothing.

But remember that past performance is not a guarantee of future results.

4.   **Put it on automatic.** Do not trust yourself to remember to make a contribution to your Roth IRA or Financial Fortress account. By setting up an automatic payment to these accounts from your checking or savings account, you are increasing the likelihood that you will build wealth over time to support your future retirement. While I am not advocating a "set it and forget it" attitude, I am very aware that some of us lack financial discipline.

** source: Dalbar

If you can set up a structure that does the work for you, you can benefit from the periodic transfers to your retirement accounts while not having to remember to take action. Ask the personnel at your bank or credit union to help you set up an automatic monthly transfer. Your financial institution will generally give you the ability to change the amount or stop it at any time.

"Systematic investing will pay off ultimately, regardless of when it is begun, provided that it is adhered to conscientiously and courageously under all market conditions."

BENJAMIN GRAHAM
Father of Value Investing

It might be nice to invest several thousand dollars each month; however, few of us are in a position to do so. With an automatic investment strategy in place, you can invest small amounts each month.*** Let's say you

---

*** ROTH IRA owners must be 59½ or older and have held the IRA for 5 years before tax-free withdrawals are permitted. Matching contributions from your employer may be subject to a vesting schedule. Please review your plan documents with your financial advisor for more information. Additionally, not every employer-sponsored retirement plan may offer matching contributions, or their matching contribution policy may

invest $250 per month into whatever investment your financial planner may have recommended. By investing the same amount each month, you are, in effect, "*dollar cost averaging.*" Very simply, when prices in the marketplace are low, your monthly investment of $250 purchases more shares. When prices are higher, you will be purchasing fewer shares. But the idea is that this will average out over a long period of time. The last thing you want to do is to try to time each investment.

I do not want you watching CNBC or any of the talking heads on competing cable channels. Keep it simple. Let compounding and time be your friend by investing regularly and periodically. You might decide to have funds transferred from your checking account to your Roth IRA on the 15th of each month, for example. You might also transfer a similar amount to your Financial Fortress monthly. The dollar amounts are not as important as instilling the behavior so that it becomes a routine. You can always increase the amounts over time, which I highly recommend. Let me say that again: do

---

differ from the example provided. Please review your retirement plans documents for more information.

not choose a dollar amount and forget it. Actively seek to raise the amount of dollars you are contributing. You do not want five years to pass by and realize that you have not increased your contributions.

5.   We have all heard the saying *"Pay yourself first."* My question to you is: are you doing this? You will accumulate far more assets in the next decade if you make investing a priority rather than an afterthought. Note I said that *investing* must be a priority, not *savings*. Think for a moment: have you ever known anyone who has become wealthy by investing in a savings account at his or her local bank? The answer is most likely no.

People become wealthy by investing in assets that have the ability to grow over time—whether shares of publicly traded companies that you have known all your life or real estate like the home in which you may have grown up. There are many investment opportunities that have the potential to earn a higher return than a savings account. You will want to engage your advisors for advice on how best to invest your funds. Remember that when you are investing for your future retirement, it is very different from holding several thousand dollars in a credit union account while you save for your next car.

I want you to think long term. The security that you will require if you expect to enjoy a lifestyle-sustaining income over a potential multi- decade period of time will, by necessity, involve a growing stream of income. Because your retirement is (hopefully) a long-term proposition, you may wish to gravitate to long-term investments.

I am a great believer in owning baskets of common stock of the global giants that make up the largest and best-capitalized corporations. I will not name these companies here, as it is enough to simply say that you buy their toothpaste, shaving cream, soap, food, tires, and gasoline. You fly planes with engines they manufacture, and you run programs using the software and computers they create. You communicate using their devices. You safeguard your money in their banks and use their checking account services as well as their debit and credit cards. These same companies provide loans so you can purchase a home for your family. The products these companies manufacture for our armed forces defend our country and many of our allies.

Many of these companies provide their owners (shareholders) with periodic cash dividends. When I reflect on the level of dividend income that has been generated by these companies for their shareholders over long periods of time, many even over decades, I see an unmistakable trend. I see income rising over long periods, often in excess of the rate of inflation.

In planning for a long-term retirement, I want my investment income to keep up with the increases in my cost of living. Ideally, I would want my income to greatly exceed the increase in my day-to-day costs. Perhaps this has given you food for thought during these volatile times in our economy.*****

***** This information is not a complete summary or statement of all available data necessary for making an investment decision and does not constitute a recommendation to buy or sell any security. Investing involves risk; investors may incur a profit or loss regardless of the strategy or strategies employed. Dollar-cost averaging cannot guarantee a profit or protect against loss. You should consider your financial ability to continue purchases through periods of low price levels. Dividends are subject to change and are not guaranteed. Dividends must be authorized by a company's board of directors.

ACTION STEPS:

1. Take a clean sheet of paper and write down all action steps you can reasonably begin to implement in the next 30 days.

2. Circle the three most important items to you and begin implementation in the next seven days.

3. Jot down three people who may be *mentor material* and think about what you would say to them. Remember that you are interviewing them for a position of great trust and responsibility!

Author's Afterword

Throughout these chapters, I have provided a blueprint to help shift your attitudes and behaviors. My hope is that this book will be your personal tipping point to propel you to take massive actions that you are not now taking. Your success or failure will be your own completely. I'm here to give you a much-needed shove. I hope what you have read in these pages has fundamentally changed your current thinking about how you will fund your retirement and the various possibilities of funding vehicles. I suggest you refer back to these pages often to reinforce the lessons I have provided.

Remember, I stated that people who successfully prepare for retirement are very different from those who don't. You see, of all the actions that need to be taken for a financially successful retirement, no one really wants to do them. The difference is that the successful people do them anyway because they know it will increase their odds of a positive outcome. Others, well, they just play the lottery and continue to hope for the day when they will win big. They do not take personal responsibility and the willingness to engage in needed actions is absent.

Retirement mindset winner!

The issue of investing for your future retirement – the day that your paychecks stop – has tremendous potential economic consequences for you. You must focus on what is important, and not remain fixated on the unimportant details that have little consequence. If your finely-honed skill is drinking coffee and reading the paper, you have a problem. In the final analysis, you must work to manufacture a synthetic paycheck; my recommendation is that you best get started.

I have known hundreds of people that prepared successfully for retirement during both good times and bad, so I infer that it does not matter whether the times are good or bad; rather, it is all about your mindset and whether or not you are going to accomplish the goal. Unfortunately, the study ethic has evaporated in many people. Many leave college or high school and are determined not to pick up books anymore.

Above all, you must place a high value on identifying and gathering information that can move you to ever-higher levels of prosperity. Whether the information is contained in an e-book, a paper volume, video or audio does not matter. What matters is that you find and digest important information that will move you forward. I implore you to create your own retirement by design, rather than agreeing to accept whatever happens by default.

Do not let this book be the end of your journey to financial awareness, but the beginning. Whether you stroll through your neighborhood bookstore or search offerings on Amazon, do not procrastinate. I suggest you get to it now, not next month or next year. For a list of additional books I have found very useful, please see the resource section in this book.

I have done my best to make sure this book has useful and accurate information.

I wish for you a long life filled with great joy and financial abundance. May you accumulate more assets than you will ever need so you can pass on what you do not use to help future generations of your family.

Other Books by Rodger A Friedman

Forging Bonds of Steel: *How to Build a Successful and Lasting Relationship with your Financial Advisor* explores how you may form a strong, trusting and lasting relationship with your financial advisor. Deep trust develops only over time, and it starts with getting to know each other. An advisor's first inquiry should be "Tell me about your family."

Richard Watts, attorney and author of *Fables of Fortune: What Rich People Have that You Don't Want* says, "An advisor must put himself at risk with honesty to the client to be effective. Rodger hits the nail on the head about the sacred nature of the client-advisor relationship."

David Darst, former Chief Investment Strategist of Morgan Stanley Wealth Management says, "With extraordinary clarity, pragmatism, insight, and emotional intelligence, Rodger Friedman masterfully provides a highly useful set of tools and common-sense advice to optimize the all-important relationship with your financial advisor."

Forging Bonds of Steel is available by visiting RodgeronRetirement.com or Amazon.com.

Fire Your Retirement Planner: You! is intended to inspire the hard-working middle-class worker to seriously consider, perhaps for the first time, that a comfortable retirement will likely be *impossible* unless he or she makes some fairly big behavioral changes. Each of the 52 short stories plays on a theme relating to what I believe is "best practices" for a successful retirement. I discuss warnings as well as easy-to-follow paths to retirement success. Many of the principles discussed in the book, if implemented, can help propel the serious reader to a six-figure retirement income. I tried to balance storytelling, information, and warnings. Ultimately, the reader will decide whether or not I accomplished that goal.

As Peter Gruber, past chairman and CEO of Sony Pictures says, "Failure is an inevitable cul-de-sac on the road to success." If I can shift the reader's focus to a success orientation, perhaps there will be more financially successful individuals approaching retirement with a feeling of accomplishment, rather than a feeling of dread.

Fire Your Retirement Planner: You! is available by visiting RodgeronRetirement.com or Amazon.com.

Additional Resources

SUGGESTED READING LIST

- *Murray, Nick. Simple Wealth, Inevitable Wealth.* The Nick Murray Company, 2nd edition, 2004.

- *Lange, James. The ROTH Revolution*: *Pay Taxes Once and Never Again.* Morgan James Publishing, 2011.

- *Darst, David. The Little Book That Still Saves Your Assets*: *What The Rich Continue to Do to Stay Wealthy in Up and Down Markets.* Wiley, 2nd edition, 2012.

- *Milevsky, Moshe A., PhD. Are You a Stock or a Bond? Identify Your Own Human Capital for a Secure Financial Future.* FT Press, 2012.

- *Loeb, Paul. The Impossible Will Take a Little While*: *Perseverance and Hope in Troubled Times.* Basic Books, 2014.

- *Malkiel, Burton G., and Ellis, Charles. The Elements of Investing: Easy Lessons for Every Investor.* Wiley, 2nd edition, 2013.

THE 15 REASONS I HEAR MOST OFTEN FOR NOT SAVING & INVESTING FOR RETIREMENT

1. I'm saving for my kids' college education.
2. Money is tight and there is none left over at the end of the month.
3. I'm saving up for a (choose one) 2nd home, car, or boat.
4. I am paying off my student loans.
5. My car loan is eating me alive.
6. After paying my mortgage, there is no money left.
7. My taxes are too high.
8. My job doesn't pay enough.
9. I need to find a roommate to cut my expenses.
10. My employer does not offer a retirement plan.
11. Interest rates are too low to save.
12. I don't know anything about investing money.
13. I'll save when I earn more money.
14. I've got plenty of time, so I'll start later.
15. When my parents die, I'll inherit their money.

RETIREMENT PLANNING BEST PRACTICES ASSESSMENT

Take out a pen and jot down a Y for "yes" or an N for "no" next to each question.

1) _____Have you seriously considered how much you would need to live on once your paychecks stop?

2) _____Have you established, and do you contribute to, either a traditional or Roth IRA account?

3) _____Do you participate in an employer-sponsored retirement plan such as a 401(K), 403(B) or 457 plan?

4) _____If your employer provides matching contributions, do you contribute enough to receive the entire matching amount?

5) _____Have you read any books on retirement or financial planning in the last 12 months?

6) _____Have you consulted with a CPA or financial advisor about how you might improve your chances of a successful retirement outcome?

7) _____Do you know how much you need to save and invest each year for retirement?

8) _____Do you buy lottery tickets in the hope that you will win enough to live without having to work?

9) _____Do you believe that your Social Security retirement benefits will be enough for you to live comfortably?

10)_____As a rule, do you save money each month in any type of account?

SCORING KEY

10 correct answers

Perfect score! You have taken significant steps to ensure that you will enjoy a successful retirement. Your actions indicate that you are proactive and serious about retirement planning. Remember that planning for retirement is not a singular event. It takes ongoing reviews and checkups to keep you on the right path. Work with a retirement team to ensure that you continue to make the right decisions.

Six correct answers

You face challenges! There is much room for improvement, but you are making some good decisions. Understand that you need to make more good decisions. It is important that you work with a retirement professional to assist you in making the best choices possible. Start as early as possible to ensure you have the most flexibility in shaping your retirement.

Four or less correct answers

Your retirement is at risk! Like a ship heading in the wrong direction, it will take work to turn it around, but it can be done. The best advice is to admit to yourself that you need help and seek out professionals with the knowledge and experience to assist you. It is never too late to begin making good decisions.

Best possible answers:

1-Y	6-Y
2-Y	7-Y
3-Y	8-N
4-Y	9-N
5-Y	10-Y

If you would like to find out how Rodger on Retirement can be of further assistance, there are three ways to contact us. Rodger Alan Friedman is also available for limited speaking engagements at schools, charities, service organizations, associations, and corporations.

Please reach out to our team.

By telephone: 1-844-3MY-PLAN

By E-mail: info@RodgeronRetirement.com

By fax: 1-844-3MY-PLAN

There are many ways to make further use of this <u>inspiring</u> and thought-provoking book.

It can inspire and educate others, promote your brand, motivate your employees and connect to inactive clients and constituencies.

You can have a custom version of *The Mindset of Retirement Success:7 Winning Strategies to Change Your Life*

- You can build personal bonds with key constituencies, prospects, employees, customers and donors.

- Deliver a memento and keepsake of an event, celebration, conference or milestone.

- Provide the definitive thank you gift that will serve as a long-lasting reminder of your caring and interest for others.

- Show that you care about the future financial wellbeing of your organization.

It is easy to show others that you care. A book is a genuine and thoughtful gift, given by a caring person or organization. It will far outshine a promotional gift such as a hat, gym bag or shirt. A book may promote further interactions and lead to discussions that will change lives.

The Mindset of Retirement Success: 7 Winning Strategies to Change Your Life is available in <u>bulk quantities</u> and in customized versions to suit your needs at <u>special discounts</u> for institutions, organizations, educational and corporate purposes. To learn more, please contact my team.

By telephone 1-844-3MY-PLAN

By E-mail at <u>info@RodgeronRetirement.com</u>

By Fax 1-844-3MY-PLAN

Rodger Friedman, CRPC®
Managing Director, Wealth Manager
Steward Partners Global Advisory
7550 Wisconsin Avenue, Suite 240
Bethesda, MD 20814
Direct: 240-800-3434
Toll-Free: 844-207-0472

"It is imperative that you grasp every opportunity you can to invest for your future retirement. Accordingly, you must contribute a portion of every paycheck to your retirement plan, regardless of whether or not your employer contributes anything at all. Bosses may come and go, and you may work at several companies throughout your career, but the one constant is what you see when you look in the mirror.

When you look at your reflection and see who looks back at you, you will come face-to-face with the individual who bears sole responsibility for your achievement or failure. Do not make the common mistake of thinking that you have plenty of time to start saving for retirement. You do not."

RODGER ALAN FRIEDMAN

About the Author

RODGER ALAN FRIEDMAN grew up in the 1960s on the lower east side of Manhattan, the youngest in a family of 5. His dad owned and managed the family laundry that was started by Rodger's grandparents. Rodger is a product of the New York City public school system (but you should not hold that against him). Never the athlete, he divided his time between riding his bicycle, reading comic books, playing ball, riding his skateboard and watching TV.

Rodger takes great pride in the fact that famous people attended Seward Park, his high school on Delancey Street on the lower east side. Although Rodger never attended classes with Walter Mathau, Tony Curtis or Zero Mostel, he loves to say they went to "his school". After school and during many summers, Rodger worked in the family laundry. It was there that he learned about capitalism and the work he did not want to pursue as an adult.

As a political science major at a small public upstate New York college, Rodger learned that he had little respect for politics, and less for politicians. Rodger's upbringing was "entrepreneurial middle class". Dinner conversation always included classwork, lectures on acceptable behavior, the problems at the laundry and the movement of the Dow Jones Industrial Average. Rodger felt the gentle push to figure out his path in the world. His older brother was an electrical engineer and his sister a social worker. Surely the universe had something more interesting than dirty laundry in mind for him.

Rodger's childhood ways were cut short by the death of his mother, shortly before he turned 13. Soon, he was the one making shopping trips to the grocery, and attending to other chores that were never part of his earlier life. He found he needed to grow up faster than he had intended.

After graduating college and moving to Queens, New York, with his college roommate, he landed his first non- laundry related job. He found his 6 months of being a real estate agent trainee to be less than inspiring. He spent his days surveying midtown Manhattan office space and learning which hotels had the coldest air conditioning and fanciest rest rooms.

Fate drew him to the New York Times classified ads and he found himself a new career on Wall Street. Rodger took great interest in the securities industry; he became part of a team at a giant brokerage firm that performed compliance audits of brokerage branch offices across the nation.

After 2 years questioning and reviewing the stockbrokers in scores of branch offices, Rodger moved to Washington, D.C. and became Operations Manager of a large brokerage office. After 2 years, he became bored with the sameness of the issues he faced on a daily basis, and applied to the financial advisor training program. It was in the Fall of 1984 that Rodger became a financial adviso

Rodger   @Rod-
geronReti   1-844-
3MY-PLA   ‿   ‿   naging
Director and Wealth Advisor at Steward Partners Global Advisory, a firm affiliated with Raymond James Financial Services.

Why This Is A
Big Deal To Me

As a six-year-old in 1962, I remember waiting for my grandpa to show up on Thanksgiving Day with a big, golden turkey. Our family was gathered at my grandparents' apartment. My granddad was a kindly old man with thinning grey hair and a twinkle in his eye, who was completely devoted to our family. My grandparents owned a small paint supply store on East 80th Street in Manhattan, which he and my grandmother ran for decades. They didn't make much money, but it paid the rent on their apartment.

As I played with my toys, my dad and uncles gazed out the window, waiting for grandpa. Suddenly, they started shouting and ran out of the apartment. My grandfather had just suffered a massive heart attack and collapsed and died on the sidewalk. The turkey was scattered around him. I saw all this unfold through the upstairs window and remember gripping the arm of the plastic covered couch with all my strength, trying to remain steady, while all around me everyone was shouting.

Shortly after grandpa died, grandma was forced to close the store. She was unable to run it herself. I remember, every Saturday morning, my dad sat down at the small mahogany desk in the living room and wrote her a check for $115. My grandma did not have enough income to survive. This check allowed her to remain in the apartment that she and grandpa had lived in for 50 years.

My father wrote the checks because he loved her and did not want to see her struggle. Grandma had already dealt with so much adversity in her life and did not need more. She fled Poland during the beginning of the Nazi occupation and was very lucky to reach America. She lost her country to Hitler, lost her husband to a heart attack, and lost her livelihood – the paint store.

I watched Dad hand grandma that check week after week, year after year and, even at that young age, I felt that it was wrong for parents to have to accept money each week from their children. This left a huge impression on me, and it motivates me to this day.

I grew up, went to college, and studied political science and economics.

After college, I took a job with a giant brokerage firm as an internal auditor. My responsibilities included interviewing stockbrokers from all over the country to make sure they followed regulations from the company, the SEC, and other government agencies.

This task led to a second defining moment that helped focus and change the direction of my life. I was in the Southwest, interviewing a young broker, about 30 years old. He was a cocky fellow, anxious to get back to trading his client accounts and clearly annoyed at me—the ops guy from New York who was interrupting his day.

I noticed that he wouldn't make eye contact with me as I questioned him. As we made our way through the interview, it quickly became clear that he was lying to me. He sat there explaining his trading strategy, telling me how he was performing a great service for his clients. But it was dawning on me that he was churning his clients' accounts, trading excessively to enrich himself at their expense. He was the sort of stockbroker I was trained to spot, document, and report to my superiors.

Sitting there, listening to him lie, I remained outwardly calm while seething inside. I wanted to scream at him for staining the honor of our firm, acting dishonestly and lying to his clients. How many regulations and laws did he break? All to put another buck in his pocket! He was hurting the very people who trusted him with their financial lives.

I decided then that I could learn to manage retirement funds. But, unlike that broker, I would do it ethically and with heart. I would guide clients as to how to structure their finances for a successful and financially rewarding retirement. I would make a difference in their lives so that they would not have to rely on their children to make ends meet, as did my grandma all those years ago.

That is why I do what I do—why I am passionate and focused on helping families make the best decisions possible for a successful and secure retirement.

Made in the USA
Columbia, SC
07 April 2023